W9-CZA-261

The New Gnu Knew

amicus readers

by Rebecca Felix

Ideas for Parents and Teachers

Amicus Readers let children practice reading informational texts at the earliest reading levels. Familiar words and concepts with close photo-text matches support early readers.

Before Reading
- Discuss the cover photo with the child. What does it tell him?
- Ask the child to predict what she will learn in the book.

Read the Book
- "Walk" through the book and look at the photos. Let the child ask questions.
- Read the book to the child, or have the child read independently.

After Reading
- Use the matching quiz at the end of the book to review the text.
- Prompt the child to make connections. Ask: *Can you think of other words that sound the same but have different meanings and spellings?*

Amicus Readers are published by Amicus
P.O. Box 1329, Mankato, MN 56002
www.amicuspublishing.us

Library of Congress Cataloging-in-Publication Data

Felix, Rebecca, 1984-
  The new gnu knew / By Rebecca Felix.
    pages cm. -- (Hear homophones here)
  Audience: K to Grade 3.
  Audience: Age 6
  ISBN 978-1-60753-570-6 (hardcover) --
  ISBN 978-1-60753-654-3 (pdf ebook)
  1. English language--Homonyms--Juvenile literature.
2. Zoo animals--Juvenile literature. I. Title.
  PE1595.F43 2014
  428.1--dc23
                          2013048622

Photo Credits: Marcelle Robbins/Shutterstock Images, cover, 1; Natali Glado/Shutterstock Images, 3; Dmitry Evteev/Dreamstime, 4–5; Adrian Hughes/Shutterstock Images, 7 (bottom), 16 (middle left); Art Allianz/Shutterstock Images, 7 (top), 16 (middle left); age fotostock/SuperStock, 8; Poznukhov Yuriy/Shutterstock Images, 10–11; Ivansabo/Dreamstime, 12; Pete Spiro/Shutterstock Images, 13, 16 (top right); James Hager/Robert Harding Picture Library/SuperStock, 14–15; Shutterstock Images, 16 (middle right); Creatas Images/Thinkstock, 16 (bottom right); Wavebreak Media/Thinkstock, 16 (top left); Fuse/Thinkstock, 16 (bottom left)

Produced for Amicus by The Peterson Publishing Company and Red Line Editorial.

Editor Jenna Gleisner
Designer Jake Nordby
Printed in the United States of America
Mankato, MN
2-2014
PA10001
10 9 8 7 6 5 4 3 2 1

Homophones are words that sound the same. But they have different meanings and spellings. What homophones can we find at the zoo?

3

4

knew
new
gnu

Workers at the zoo **knew** it would be an exciting day. People were coming to see the **new gnu**.

bye
by
buy

Aida and Ian say to their parents, "**Bye**!" They get to the zoo **by** riding their bikes. They **buy** tickets at the gates.

SAFARI AFRICA

TAMPA'S LOWRY PARK ZOO

they're
their
there

Aida and Ian enter the zoo. **They're** meeting **their** friends over **there** by the elephant.

rode
road
rowed

The friends **rode** a trolley. It took a **road** past the pond. Zoo workers **rowed** a boat into the pond. They fed the alligators.

scent
cent
sent

Next, Aida smelled the **scent** of fish. Fish to feed the seals were sold for one **cent** each. Aida **sent** Ian to buy fish.

two
to
too

The **two** friends saw many animals. At last, they went **to** see the new gnu, **too**!

Match each homophone to its picture!

road

rowed

scent

cent

buy

bye